AQA GCSE MATHS

FOUNDATION

Steve Cavill
Geoff Gibb

EXAM PRACTICE BOOK

Powered by  MyMaths.co.uk

OXFORD
UNIVERSITY PRESS

OXFORD
UNIVERSITY PRESS

Great Clarendon Street, Oxford, OX2 6DP, United Kingdom

Oxford University Press is a department of the University of Oxford.
It furthers the University's objective of excellence in research,
scholarship, and education by publishing worldwide. Oxford is a
registered trade mark of Oxford University Press in the UK and in
certain other countries

British Library Cataloguing in Publication Data
Data available

978-0-19-835168-9

10 9 8 7 6 5 4 3 2 1

Paper used in the production of this book is a natural, recyclable
product made from wood grown in sustainable forests.
The manufacturing process conforms to the environmental
regulations of the country of origin.

Printed in Great Britain

Acknowledgements
Cover image: David Ashley/Shutterstock

Although we have made every effort to trace and contact all
copyright holders before publication this has not been possible in all
cases. If notified, the publisher will rectify any errors or omissions at
the earliest opportunity.

Links to third party websites are provided by Oxford in good faith
and for information only. Oxford disclaims any responsibility for
the materials contained in any third party website referenced in
this work.

1　Calculations 1

1 The numbers 12.5, 15.06, 9.9002 and 9.06 are put in order starting with the lowest.

Helen says 'Even if you round the numbers correct to 1 significant figure you will still get the same order'.

Is she correct? Explain your answer clearly. **[3 marks]**

....

....

....

....

....

2 A, 7.5 and C are three numbers.

There is a difference of 5.8 between A, the highest number, and C, the lowest number.

7.5 is exactly halfway between A and C.

Find A and C. **[3 marks]**

....

....

....

....

$A =$ _____　　$C =$ _____

3 An integer, G, is rounded to give the value 10 000.

a Write down a possible value for G. **[1 mark]**

Answer _____

b Find the greatest possible difference between values for G. **[3 marks]**

....

....

....

....

Answer _____

4   Gemma adds two integers; the answer is 19.

She says 'The difference between my numbers is 5.'

What are Gemma's two numbers?

Show that your answer is correct.   **[2 marks]**

....

....

....

....

....

....

Answer _____ and _____

5   In this question the year is 2015 and you can only use each digit of the date once in your answer to part **b**.

Ali says 'I can make a calculation with the answer 10.'

He writes

$$10 - 5 \times 2 = 10$$

and says

10 take away 5 is 5

5 times 2 is 10.

a   Explain why Ali is wrong and give the correct answer to the calculation.   **[2 marks]**

....

....

....

....

b   Write two different calculations each with the answer 10.   **[2 marks]**

....

....

Answer _____ and _____

6 Airlines have these rules about the size of bags that can be carried on to a plane.

A bag must have length < 56 cm   and

width < 45 cm   and

depth < 25 cm.

Jenny's bag has a depth of 24 cm.

The area of the front of the case is 2200 cm².

Sean says 'You won't be able to carry that case on to a plane.'

Jenny thinks she will be able to.

Show that Sean and Jenny could both be correct.   **[5 marks]**

Area of front = length × width

....

....

....

....

....

....

....

....

....

....

....

....

7   Decide whether each statement is *always* true, *sometimes* true or *never* true.

In each case, give an example to support your answer.

a   A number P, correct to the nearest integer, is 5.

Another number Q, correct to 1 decimal place, is 5.0.

So $P \neq Q$.   [2 marks]

The statement is _____ true.

Example ....

....

....

....

b G is an integer and $0 \leq H \leq 1$.

$$\frac{G}{H} > G$$ [2 marks]

The statement is _____ true.

Example ....

....

....

....

2 Expressions

1 In a magic square the total of every row, every column and every diagonal is the same.
In a normal magic square the numbers used are the integers 1, 2, 3, …

4	9	2
3	5	7
8	1	6

Total = 15

Here is a 4-by-4 magic square.

7	12	1	14
2	13	8	11
16	3	10	5
9	6	15	4

The total, T, for a normal magic square with n squares on each side is $T = \dfrac{n(n^2 + 1)}{2}$.

a Show that this formula gives the correct total for the 4-by-4 square shown. **[2 marks]**

....

....

....

....

b This is a 2-by-2 square.

g	

Write expressions in terms of g for each of the remaining three squares,
and decide whether it is possible to have a 2-by-2 normal magic square. **[4 marks]**

....

....

....

....

....

....

2 The shape of the Earth is an oblate spheroid.

The formula for its volume is

$$V = \frac{4}{3}\pi a^2 c$$

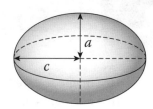

where

- a is the polar radius (distance between the centre and the North Pole)
- c is the equatorial radius (distance between the centre and the equator).

a The internet gives the following information for the Earth.

Polar diameter (distance between N and S poles) = 7900 miles.
Equatorial diameter is 26 miles more than the polar diameter.

Show that the volume of the earth is **approximately** 260 billion cubic miles. **[4 marks]**

....

....

....

....

....

....

....

b A silver ornament is made in the shape of an oblate spheroid with $a = 3c$.
Find an expression for its volume in terms of c. **[3 marks]**

....

....

....

....

....

....

Answer _____

3 Here *a* is a whole number.

You are given three facts about a rectangle:

- The length of the rectangle is a whole-number multiple of *a*.
- The width of the rectangle is a whole number.
- The area of the rectangle is $12a^2 + 6a$.

a Find all **four** different pairs of values for the length and width of the rectangle. **[4 marks]**

....

....

....

....

....

Answer _____

_____

b An expression for the perimeter of the rectangle is $14a + k$.

Find the value of the integer *k*. **[2 marks]**

....

....

....

....

....

Answer _____

4 **a** Ethan says that $4^{x+4} = 2^{x+6}$ because $4 = 2^2$.

Explain why Ethan is wrong and write 4^{x+4} as a power of 2. **[2 marks]**

....

....

....

....

....

Answer _____

b Find the value of x. **[4 marks]**

$$\frac{2^{12x-3} \times 4^{x+4}}{2^{5+13x}} = 2^5$$

....

....

....

....

....

....

....

....

....

....

....

....

....

....

....

....

3 Angles and polygons

1 The diagram is drawn using a square and two congruent rhombuses.

Shapes join full edge to full edge.

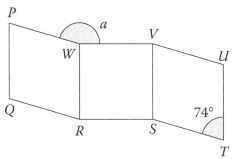

Not to scale

Bryn finds the value of *a*.

$\angle UTS = \angle WRQ = 74°$ Corresponding angles in rhombus

$\angle PWR = 180° - 74° = 116°$ Alternate angles between parallel lines

$\angle RWV = 90°$ Angles in a square

$\therefore a = 360° - 90° - 116° = 154°$ Angles at a point add up to 360°

Bryn has made some mistakes.

Rewrite the working, correcting the errors and underlining the changes you make.   **[3 marks]**

....

....

....

2 a This represents a 1 cm square grid.

Draw four more straight lines to create four congruent shapes that are not squares.

Each line must start from the end of an existing line and finish on the perimeter of the outer square.   **[2 marks]**

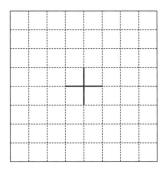

b What is the area of each congruent part?   **[2 marks]**

....

....

....

Answer _____ cm²

3 $AB = AD$ and $CB = CD$

BDE is a straight line.

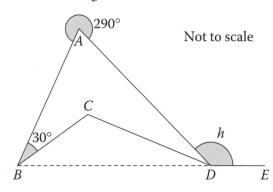

290°

A

Not to scale

C

30°

h

B

D

E

Find the value of *h*, identifying any angles found in the process.

Give reasons for any two of the angles you find.

[6 marks]

....

....

....

....

....

....

....

....

....

....

$h = $ _____°

4 Two of these isosceles trapeziums are joined whole edge to whole edge to form a polygon.

a Sketch all the polygons you can make from two of these trapeziums. **[3 marks]**

b Can any of these polygons be regular?
Explain your answer fully. **[4 marks]**

....

....

....

....

....

....

....

....

....

5 **a** A rectangle, *PQRS*, has one diagonal, *QS*, drawn.

Complete this proof that triangle *SPQ* is congruent to triangle *QRS*. **[3 marks]**

SQ is a common side.

Angle *SPQ* ....

PQ ....

Therefore triangle *SPQ* is congruent to triangle *QRS* because ....

b The diagram shows a plan view of a model plane.
Angles in corresponding positions in the front and rear wings are equal.

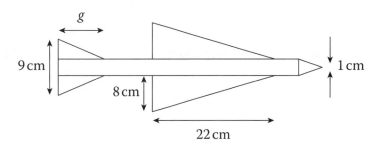

Find g, the length of the rear wing. **[2 marks]**

....

....

....

....

....

Answer _____ cm

4 Handling data 1

1 The incomplete bar graph and pie chart each show the same information about the number of bikes each person in a group of people has ever owned.

Number of bikes owned

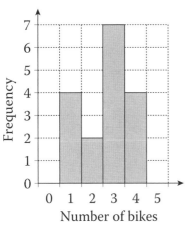

Number of bikes owned

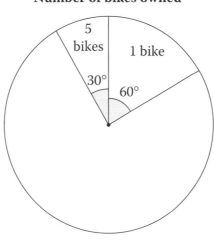

Complete the pie chart. [6 marks]

....

....

....

....

....

....

....

....

....

....

....

....

....

....

2 Anya asks the first 20 people who come into her sweet shop about their favourite type of sweet. Her results are summarised in the table.

Type of sweet	Frequency
Gobstoppers	3
Refreshers	5
Bubble gum	6
Liquorice laces	11
Milk bottles	12

a How can you tell that some people answer with more than one type of sweet? **[1 mark]**

Answer _____

Anya wants to present her results as a diagram.

b Choose an appropriate form of presentation and represent Anya's data. **[2 marks]**

3 All of these measures apply to a single set of five integers.
- Mode = 2
- Median = 2
- Mean = 3
- Range = 3

Find this set of five numbers. **[3 marks]**

....

....

....

....

....

Answer _____

4 Barry conducts a survey about the number of bedrooms people have in their homes.

He surveyed 20 people, each living in a different home.

The modal number of bedrooms was 3.

The smallest number of bedrooms was 1.

The range was 6.

The number of people living in 2-bedroomed homes was 1 less than the number living in homes with the modal number of bedrooms.

No one lived in a home with 5 bedrooms.

Use the axes to draw a possible bar chart to show Barry's results.

Label the axes. **[7 marks]**

Number of bedrooms

....

....

....

....

....

5   Lizzie is in Year 13. She carries out a survey to find out how many of her classmates drive.

She collects the following information.

- There are 200 students in Y13.
- 70 of the boys drive.
- 80 students do not drive.
- There are same number of girls who drive as boys who do not drive.

a   How many students drive?   **[1 mark]**

....

Answer _____

b   Complete the two-way table.   **[3 marks]**

	Drive	Do not drive	Total
Boys			
Girls			
Total			

c   Scarlett says that there is a bigger fraction of girls who are drivers than drivers who are girls. Is Scarlett correct? Explain your answer.   **[2 marks]**

....

....

....

Answer _____

5 Fractions, decimals and percentages

1 Gerry has a bag of sweets.

He keeps $\frac{1}{2}$ of the sweets for himself, gives $\frac{1}{4}$ of the sweets to his sister and gives 50% of the remaining sweets to Ruby.

There are 3 sweets left.

How many sweets were in the bag at the start? **[3 marks]**

....

....

....

....

....

....

....

Answer _____

2 You are given that $\frac{1}{3} + \frac{a}{b} = \frac{7}{12}$.

Find the lowest value of a and the lowest value of b. **[2 marks]**

....

....

....

....

....

....

....

$a =$ _____

$b =$ _____

3 Three shops each sell the same make of shirt for the same price.

Each shop has a sale.

| Allan's 35% off | TIP-TOP Buy one get the second half price | Perry $\frac{1}{3}$ off |

Dan buys two shirts in one of the shops.

In which shop will he get the best deal?

Show how you decide.   **[5 marks]**

....

....

....

....

....

....

....

                                                         Answer _____

4 Branka asked all the members of her year group if they preferred dogs to cats.

She found

- 0.6 preferred dogs

- $\frac{3}{10}$ did not prefer dogs

- 15% did not know.

Could Branka's results be correct? Show how you decide.   **[2 marks]**

....

....

....

....

....

                                                         Answer _____

5 Does the regular hexagon or the square have the greater fraction shaded?

The centre of each shape is marked with a dot.

Use fractions to show how you decide.

[5 marks]

....

....

....

....

....

....

....

....

....

....

....

....

....

....

....

....

Answer _____

6 40% of g is 8 more than 0.35 of g.

Find the value of g. **[4 marks]**

....

....

....

....

....

....

....

....

....

$g =$ _____

7 A fraction is in the form $\frac{1}{a}$ where a is an integer between 1 and 10.

A number divided by this fraction is 50.

The same number multiplied by this fraction is 2.

What is the fraction? **[4 marks]**

....

....

....

....

....

....

....

....

Answer _____

6 Formulae and functions

1 This is a method to change lengths in feet and inches into metres.

Step 1: multiply the number of feet in the measurement, f, by 12

Step 2: add the number of inches in the measurement, i, to the answer in Step 1

Step 3: multiply the sum by 2.5

Step 4: divide the answer by 100

a Joel is 5 feet 9 inches tall.
Use the method to show that Joel's height is 1.725 metres. **[1 mark]**

....

....

....

b Body Mass Index, *BMI*, is a way to tell if someone is at a healthy weight.
This is a formula to calculate *BMI*.

$$BMI = \frac{m}{h^2}$$

Where

- m is a person's mass in kilograms
- h is a person's height in metres.

A person has a healthy weight if their $BMI \leq 25$. | 1 pound (lb) = 0.45 kg |

Ruben is 6 feet 1 inch tall and weighs 165 lb.

Is Ruben at a healthy weight? **[6 marks]**

....

....

....

....

....

....

....

....

....

....

2 If a right-angled triangle has three sides whose lengths are whole numbers, then those three numbers are known as a Pythagorean triple. This question investigates ways of forming Pythagorean triples.

a Let $m = 2$ and $n = 1$. Calculate

    i $2mn$ **[1 mark]**

....

Answer _____

    ii $m^2 - n^2$ **[1 mark]**

....

Answer _____

    iii $m^2 + n^2$ **[1 mark]**

....

Answer _____

b Show that your three answers in part **a** satisfy Pythagoras' theorem, $a^2 + b^2 = c^2$.   **[2 marks]**

....

....

....

....

The three expressions in part **a** generate a Pythagorean triple for all positive whole number values of m and n.

c Use $m = 3$ and $n = 2$ to generate a Pythagorean triple and show that it satisfies Pythagoras' theorem.   **[4 marks]**

....

....

....

....

....

....

....

d Use the expressions from part **a** to generate a Pythagorean triple with one side as 33. **[3 marks]**

....

....

....

....

....

....

....

....

....

Answer _____

e Show that a triangle with sides $2mn$, $m^2 - n^2$ and $m^2 + n^2$ satisfies Pythagoras' theorem. **[6 marks]**

....

....

....

....

....

....

....

....

....

7 Working in 2D

1   Point *A* is plotted on the grid.

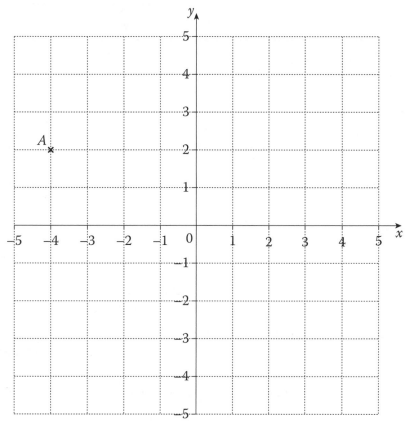

Point *A* is translated to point *B* using vector $\begin{bmatrix} p \\ q \end{bmatrix}$.

Point *B* is then translated to (4, −4) using vector $\begin{bmatrix} p \\ -4q \end{bmatrix}$.

Find the value of *p* and the value of *q*.   **[4 marks]**

....

....

....

....

....

....

p = _____ and *q* = _____

2 Triangle *ABC* is drawn on this square grid.

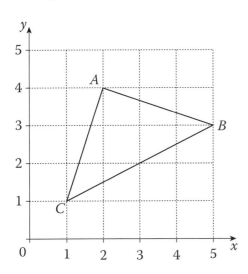

Without measuring, explain why triangle *ABC* is isosceles but not equilateral. **[3 marks]**

....

....

....

....

....

3 The parallelogram and the triangle have the same area.

They also have the same height.

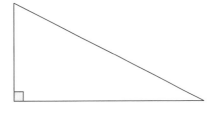

6.5 cm

Area = 60 cm²

10 cm

Find the length of the base of the triangle. **[4 marks]**

....

....

....

....

....

....

Length of triangle's base = _____ cm

4   A triangle and a square are drawn on a grid.

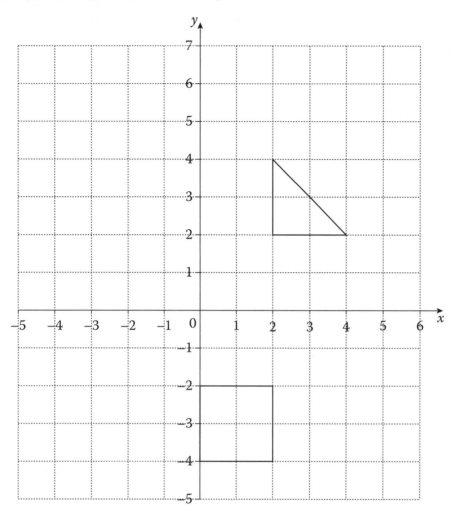

The triangle is transformed using a single transformation.

The square is also transformed using a single transformation.

The two images do not overlap and they form a trapezium.

The transformations used are a rotation and a reflection.

Draw the trapezium and describe the two transformations fully.   **[4 marks]**

....

....

....

The _____ is reflected _____.

....

....

....

The _____ is rotated _____.

5 The length, width and area of a rectangle are shown.

Each of the measurements is metric but no units are included.

Complete the statement by writing in the units used and show that your values give the correct answer.

> Area = 7.2   width = 1.2
>
> length = 60

[4 marks]

The length is 60 _____, the width is 1.2 _____ and the area is 7.2 _____.

....

....

....

....

....

....

6 The line *AC* is the hypotenuse of a right-angled triangle, *ABC*, whose other two sides are horizontal and vertical.

Triangle *ABC* is an enlargement of triangle *PQR* drawn using a scale factor of 2 and centre (−3, −2).

AB corresponds to *PR*.

Write down the possible coordinates of *Q*.

[6 marks]

....

....

....

....

(_____ , _____) and (_____ , _____)

8 Probability

In questions 1b, 2 and 3 give your answer as a fraction in its simplest form.

1 Lucy makes a target for a dart using this square grid.

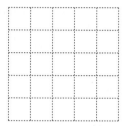

She colours whole squares either black or white.

a Explain why she cannot make a target in which

Probability of hitting a black square = Probability of hitting a white square. **[2 marks]**

....

....

....

....

....

b Write down the probability, using this target, that is closest to

Probability of hitting a black square = Probability of hitting a white square. **[1 mark]**

....

....

....

....

....

Answer _____

2   Estimate the probability that the next person you meet will have the average number of people in their family.

Explain your reasoning and any assumptions you make.   **[3 marks]**

....

....

....

....

....

                                                    Answer _____

3   In this question, give each probability as a fraction in its simplest form.

A set of dominoes consists of 28 tiles numbered blank-blank, blank-1, blank-2, ... up to blank-6, then 1-1, 1-2, ... up to 1-6 and so on up to 6-6.

a   Jayne draws a domino at random from a full set.
    Find the probability that

    i   it contains at least one 4

                                                                              [2 marks]

....

....

                                                    Answer _____

    ii   its spots add up to at least 9.   **[3 marks]**

....

....

....

                                                    Answer _____

b Fifteen of the dominoes have an even number of dots on them altogether (not counting the blank-blank domino).

    i Jayne draws a domino at random from a full set and sees that it is a 4–6. She does not return this domino to the set.

      She now draws a second domino.

      What is the probability that this domino has an even number of dots on it? **[2 marks]**

      ....

      ....

      ....

      Answer _____

    ii In a different experiment, Jayne draws a domino at random from a full set and records if it has an even number of dots on it. Then she returns the domino to the set. She does this 70 times.

      How many times should she expect to get a domino with an even number of dots on it? **[3 marks]**

      ....

      ....

      ....

      Answer _____

c Stanley says that the probability of drawing a domino at random from a full set and getting a domino with an odd number of dots on it must be $1 - \dfrac{15}{28} = \dfrac{13}{28}$.

   Explain why Stanley is wrong. **[2 marks]**

   ....

   ....

   ....

   ....

   Answer _____

   _____

   _____

4   Lianne has a fair, circular spinner with red, green, blue, yellow and black sectors.

There is a 15% chance of landing on red.

The probability of landing on green is $\frac{1}{4}$ and the probability of landing on blue is $\frac{3}{10}$.

The spinner is 100% more likely to land on black than yellow.

a   Complete this table of sector angles used to make the spinner.   **[6 marks]**

Colour	Sector angle
Red	
Green	
Blue	108°
Yellow	
Black	

....

....

....

....

....

....

....

....

....

....

....

....

....

....

b   Explain why the spinner can be called fair when the probability of landing
on each colour is different.   **[1 mark]**

....

....

....

9 Measures and accuracy

1 a Gemma shares £70 between her three children.

She works out $3\overline{)70}$ and gets the answer 23.33333333 .

Can Gemma share all the £70 equally between her three children?
Explain your answer fully. **[2 marks]**

....

....

....

....

b Rob walks at 6 km/h for half an hour and then rides at 24 km/h for half an hour.
Rob says
'I have travelled for an hour and covered 30 kilometres. My average speed is 30 km/h'.
Explain why Rob is wrong and give his actual average speed. **[3 marks]**

....

....

....

....

....

....

....

....

....

....

Average speed = _____ km/h

2   Lenny's car can carry a maximum total weight of 1174 pounds.
(This includes everything extra put in the car: people, fuel, etc.)

Lenny weighs 191 pounds and 1 litre of diesel weighs 0.85 kilograms.

Lenny has about 25 litres of diesel in the tank of his car.

He has to collect 985 bricks that each weigh between 2.5 and 2.7 kilograms.

A kilogram is roughly 2.2 pounds.

Use rounding to estimate the number of trips Lenny will need to make to safely
collect all the bricks.   **[5 marks]**

....

....

....

....

....

....

....

....

....

....

....

....

....

Answer _____

3 The digits of the date 2015 are each used once in a calculation.

The symbols +, −, ×, ÷ and ( ) can be used.

Examples are $2 + 0 + 1 - 5$ and $50 - 21$.

Find five different calculations each with the answer 5.

Different calculations must have different symbols between numbers and not just a different order.

For example:

$2 + 0 + 1 - 5$ and $2 - 5 + 0 + 1$ are **not** different (same numbers and symbols reordered).

$2 + 0 + 1 - 5$ and $2 + 0 + 1 \times 5$ are different ($- 5$ has changed to $\times 5$)   **[4 marks]**

....

....

....

....

....

Answer _____

_____

_____

_____

_____

4 A rectangle is four times as long as it is wide.

The perimeter is 80 cm correct to the nearest centimetre.

Calculate the minimum possible length of the rectangle.   **[3 marks]**

....

....

....

....

Answer _____ cm

5 The density of gold is 19.3 g/cm³.

The diameter of an Olympic medal is 60 mm.

Pure gold costs £24 000 for 1 kg.

302 gold medals were won at the 2012 Olympic Games in London.

By finding the cost of a layer of gold, 0.5 mm thick, on one face of one medal, estimate the cost of coating both faces of all the medals with gold.

[8 marks]

> You may find this information helpful:
>
> Volume of a prism
>
> V = area of cross-section × length
>
> Area of a circle
>
> $A = \pi r^2$
>
> π is approximately 3.142

....

....

....

....

....

....

....

....

....

....

....

....

....

....

....

....

....

....

£ _____

10   Equations and inequalities

1   Gina's flight time is h hours.

The time she waits in the airport is equal to half the flight time.

Gina spends a total of 6 hours waiting and flying.

a   Show that $3h = 12$.   **[2 marks]**

....

....

....

b   Solve the equation in part **a** and find how long
Gina waited in the airport.   **[2 marks]**

....

....

....

....

Answer _____ hours

2   Ian goes to the supermarket.

He chooses 3 apples from a box.

Next he buys 2 bags of apples. The number of apples in each bag is x.

Altogether he has fewer than 17 apples.

a   Write an inequality in x and solve it to find the greatest number of apples in a bag.   **[3 marks]**

....

....

....

Answer _____

b   Show the **solutions** to your **inequality** on this number line.   **[1 mark]**

0   1   2   3   4   5   6   7   8   9   10

3 Here is part of the graph of $y = x^2$.

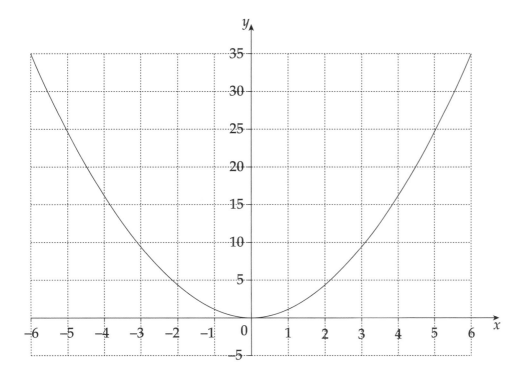

A square has an area of 23 cm².

Use the graph to work out the distance all around the square in centimetres, correct to the nearest millimetre.

[2 marks]

....

....

....

Answer _____ cm

4 Here is a triangle.

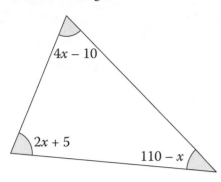

Find the value of x. **[3 marks]**

....

....

....

....

....

Answer _____

5 The area of this rectangle is $12 \, cm^2$.

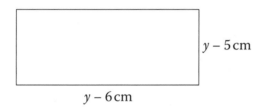

Use algebra to find the possible values of y and comment on your solutions. **[5 marks]**

....

....

....

....

....

Answer _____

_____

6 Sam collects 2 pence pieces and 5 pence pieces in a jar.

Altogether, he has 157 coins and they are worth £5.90.

Let the number of 2 pence pieces be t and the number of 5 pence pieces be f.

Form and solve a pair of simultaneous equations to find how many of each coin Sam has.   **[5 marks]**

....

....

....

....

....

....

....

....

....

Answer _____ 2p coins and _____ 5p coins

7 Here is Clinton's solution of the inequality $5 - 3x < 20$.

$5 - 3x < 20$

$-3x < 25$

$x < -\dfrac{25}{3}$

Clinton has made two errors.

Explain his errors.   **[2 marks]**

....

....

....

....

Error 1 _____

Error 2 _____

11 Circles and constructions

1 *A*, *B*, *C* and D are points on a circle.

AC and *BD* are equal in length and they are perpendicular and bisect each other.

A North line is also shown.

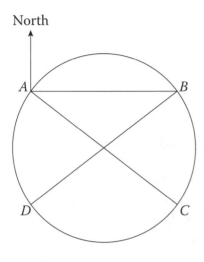

Calculate the bearing of *C* from *A*.   **[2 marks]**

....

....

....

Answer _____cm²

2 The perimeter of a square is equal to the circumference of a circle with radius 10 cm.

Find the area of the square.   **[3 marks]**

....

....

....

....

....

....

....

....

Answer _____cm²

3   A decoration is made from two circles and a square of silver.

The dots mark the centre of each circle.

The square has side length 6 cm and the decoration is 2 mm thick.

Information

Silver costs 30p per gram.

$1 cm^3$ of silver has mass 10.5 g.

To find the volume of the decoration, multiply the area of the front face in cm^2 by the thickness in cm.

Find the cost of the silver used to make the decoration.   **[7 marks]**

....

....

....

....

....

....

....

....

....

....

....

....

....

....

....

....

....

£ _____

4   Use only a pair of compasses, straight edge and pencil to answer this question.
    Do not measure any lengths and do not rub out your arcs.

    Draw a sketch to show a square with the midpoints of two adjacent sides joined.
    Draw the shape accurately.
    One side of the square has been drawn for you.   **[6 marks]**

5 The diagram shows a rectangle *ABCD*, the bisector of angle *BAD* and an arc with centre *C*.

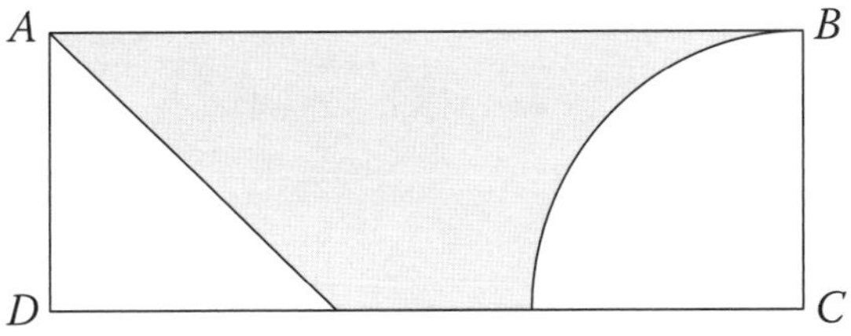

Complete this description of the shaded region. **[2 marks]**

The shaded region is the locus of points inside the rectangle that are _____

_____

_____

_____

6 The diagram shows a quarter-circle with a chord drawn.

When π is taken to have the value 3, the area
of the segment is $16\,\text{cm}^2$.

Calculate the radius of the circle. **[5 marks]**

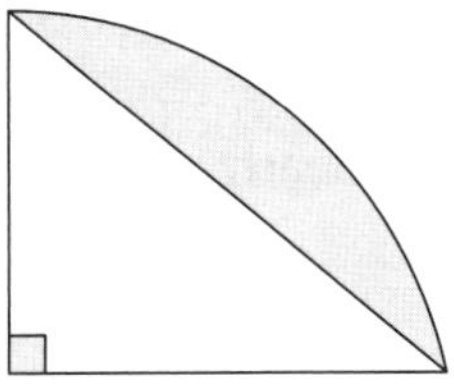

Not to scale

....

....

....

....

....

....

....

....

Answer _____ cm

12 Ratio and proportion

1 Khalid has two bags.
Bag A contains 3 red balls and 7 blue balls.
Bag B contains 2 blue balls.

Khalid takes some balls from Bag A and puts them in Bag B.
The ratio 'number of red balls : number of blue balls' is now the same in each bag.
What balls did Khalid move from Bag A to Bag B?
Show that your answer is correct.

[3 marks]

....

....

....

....

....

2 Anya has a map of Newland drawn to a scale where 1 cm represents 0.5 km.

Denny has a map of the same area drawn to a scale of 1 : 5000.

Denny says 'We should use my map because we will be able to see small details more clearly'.

Is Denny correct?

Show how you decide.

[3 marks]

....

....

....

....

....

....

....

....

....

3 **a** Rita plants her allotment in the ratio beans : potatoes = 2 : 3.

She thinks that $\frac{2}{3}$ of the plants in her allotment are beans.

Is Rita correct?

Show how you decide. **[1 mark]**

....

....

....

....

....

b Rita plants 2 kg of seed potatoes.

She finds this information about the mass of potatoes she could harvest from the seed potatoes.

Smallest mass	15 kg
Greatest mass	60 kg

She says that the smallest harvest is $\frac{2}{15}$ of the mass of the seed.

This is $\frac{2}{15} \times 100$, which is just over a 13% increase.

The biggest harvest is $\frac{2}{60} \times 100$, which is about a 3% increase.

Explain why Rita is incorrect and give the correct answers. **[3 marks]**

....

....

....

....

....

....

....

....

4 Dwayne and Julie work at the same factory. Dwayne earns £700 per month and Julie earns £800 per month.

Julie's boss gives her a pay rise of 16%.

Dwayne wants to earn the same as Julie.

Show that he can do that with a percentage pay rise that is roughly double that of Julie's. **[6 marks]**

....

....

....

....

....

....

....

....

....

....

5 Grandpa Nick invests £20 000 in an account that pays 2% simple interest each year.

At the end of each year he divides the interest earned between his three grandchildren, Alice, Beth and Connor, in the ratio of their ages.

In the year 2010 he gave Connor, who had only recently started going to school, £250, and Beth was given twice as much as Alice.

a How old was Beth in 2010?

[4 marks]

....

....

....

....

....

....

....

....

Answer _____

One year Connor will get £32 more than Alice and £24 more than Beth.

b   In what year will this happen?   **[5 marks]**

....

....

....

....

....

....

....

....

....

Answer _____

13 Factors, powers and roots

1 The Venn diagram shows the prime factors of two numbers, *A* and *B*.

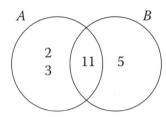

a Write down the lowest possible value of *B*. [1 mark]

....

....

Answer _____

b Explain why *A* must be an even number. [1 mark]

....

....

c Complete this statement. [1 mark]

Numbers *A* and *B* are both divisible by _____ .

....

....

d Work out a value for the product of *A* and *B* that is not the lowest possible one. [2 marks]

....

....

Answer _____

2 Tim and Elaine each think of a number.

Tim says 'My number is a cube number'.

Elaine says 'My number has an even, integer square root'.

Can they both be thinking of the same number?

Show how you decide. **[3 marks]**

....

....

....

....

....

....

....

3 Here are two lists.

Each list contains two of the multiples of an integer between 1 and 10.

Multiples of X		66			84

Multiples of Y		80				112

Find the lowest common multiple (LCM) of the numbers X and Y. **[5 marks]**

....

....

....

....

....

....

....

....

Answer _____

4 Trains arrive at the station every 5 minutes starting from 10 a.m.

Buses from the town centre arrive at the station every 6 minutes from 10 a.m. onwards.

Don gets on a bus that arrives at the station between 10 a.m. and 11 a.m.

What is the probability that Don's bus arrives at the station at the same time as a train?

Show how you decide, justifying any decisions you make. **[5 marks]**

....

....

....

....

....

....

....

....

....

....

....

Answer _____

5 **a** Write 440 as the product of its prime factors.   **[2 marks]**

....

....

....

....

....

....

....

....

....

Answer_____

b Annie has a can that holds 440 ml of liquid.

She finds that she can use all the liquid to fill a cuboid.

The internal dimensions of the cuboid are all integers.

None of the dimensions is greater than 20 cm.

Find the dimensions of all the possible cuboids.   **[5 marks]**

....

....

....

....

....

....

....

....

....

Answer _____

14 Graphs 1

1   A square is to be drawn on a 1 cm square grid.

    a   SQUARE A.

        The equations of the lines forming two of the sides are $y = -1$ and $y = 4$.

        Write two possible equations for the lines forming the other two sides.

        What is the area of the square?   **[3 marks]**

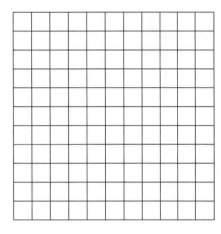

....

....

....

....

Equation 1 _____

Equation 2 _____

Area _____ cm²

    b   SQUARE B.

        The equations of the lines forming two of the sides are $y = x$ and $y = 4 - x$.

        The x-axis is a line of symmetry for the square.

        What are the equations of the lines forming the other two sides?

        What are the coordinates of the vertices of the square?

        What is the area of the square?   **[5 marks]**

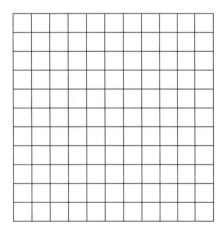

....

....

....

....

Equation 1 _____

Equation 2 _____

Vertices (____ , ____)   (____ , ____)   (____ , ____)   (____ , ____)

Area _____ cm²

2 This sketch of a distance–time graph represents Jacob's journey to school one day.

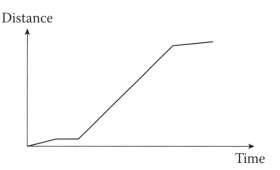

Distance

Time

Explain what each section of the graph tells us, and give one way in which the graph does not represent the real-life situation. **[5 marks]**

....

....

....

....

....

....

....

....

3 Line L has the equation $y = 4x - 7$.

a Which equation represents a line that is perpendicular to line L? **[1 mark]**

A $y = -4x + 2$	**B** $y = -\frac{1}{4}x + 2$	**C** $y = 4x + \frac{1}{7}$	**D** $y = \frac{1}{4}x + 7$

....

....

....

Answer _____

b Which equation represents a line that has the same y-intercept as line L? **[1 mark]**

A $y = -4x + 7$	**B** $y = 4$	**C** $2y = 7x - 14$	**D** $y = 4x + \frac{1}{7}$

....

....

....

Answer _____

4   This is a sketch of Alan's pursuit cycle race.

The coordinates for the turning points of the graph are shown.

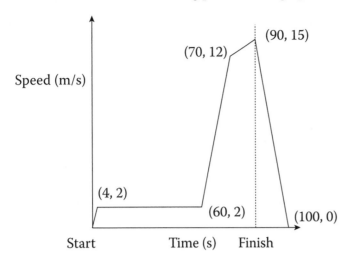

a   For how many minutes does the race last?   **[1 mark]**

....

Answer _____ minutes

b   Describe what is happening in the horizontal section of the graph.   **[1 mark]**

_____

_____

c   What is Alan's speed 6 seconds after crossing the finish line?   **[1 mark]**

....

....

Answer _____ m/s

5

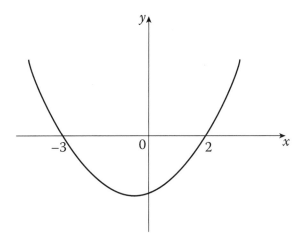

A sketch of a quadratic graph is given.

a Find a possible equation of the graph, giving your answer in the form $y = ax^2 + bx + c$. Hence use your equation to give the y-intercept of the graph. **[4 marks]**

....

....

....

....

Equation _____ y-intercept _____

b

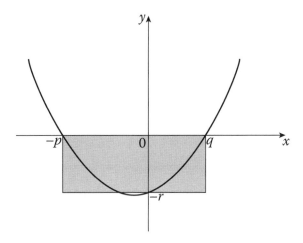

This quadratic graph has an equation of the form $y = x^2 + bx + c$.

It crosses the x-axis at $-p$ and q and the y-axis at $-r$.

The shaded rectangle has two adjacent vertices at $-p$ and q on the x-axis and its lower edge passes through $-r$ on the y-axis.

Find the area of the rectangle in terms of p and q. **[3 marks]**

....

....

....

Answer _____

15 Working in 3D

1 a A cube is cut from the corner of a cuboid.

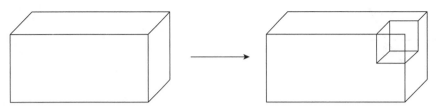

Choose from the words   increases   stays the same   decreases
to complete this statement.

The volume of the cube _____ and the surface area

of the cube _____.   **[2 marks]**

b A cuboid is cut in half.

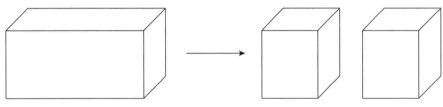

Choose from the words   increases   stays the same   decreases
to complete this statement.

The volume of the cuboid _____ and the surface area

of the cuboid _____.   **[2 marks]**

c Choose from the words   greater than   the same as   less than
to complete these statements.

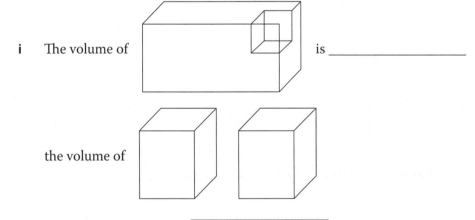

i The volume of   is _____

the volume of

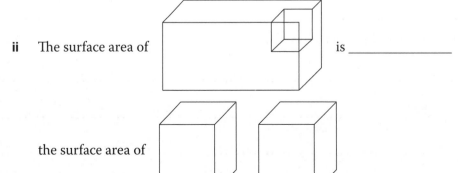

ii The surface area of   is _____

the surface area of

          [2 marks]

2 Write down the name of the solid that has one axis of symmetry and

   a   order of rotation symmetry 4   **[1 mark]**

                                     Answer _____

   b   order of rotation symmetry 2   **[1 mark]**

                                       Answer _____

   c   order of rotation symmetry infinity.   **[1 mark]**

                                       Answer _____

3 A cube has a volume that is numerically the same as its surface area.

Find the length of one edge of the cube.
What can you say about the units of your answer?   **[4 marks]**

....

....

....

....

....

....

....

....

....

....

....

             Length of edge _____

             Comment about units _____

4   This is the plan view of a solid.

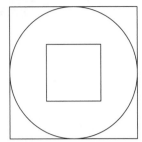

Use the grid and a ruler to draw two completely different side elevations of the solid.

Hidden edges should be drawn as dotted.

(The two elevations must **not just** have different heights.)   **[4 marks]**

5   Milk is sold in packs that are square-based prisms.

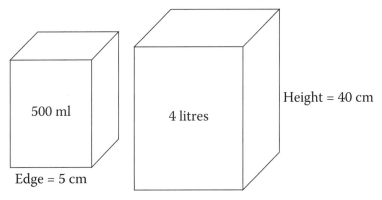

500 ml

Edge = 5 cm

4 litres

Height = 40 cm

Are the two packs mathematically similar?

Show how you decide.   **[8 marks]**

....

....

....

....

....

....

....

....

....

....

....

....

....

....

....

....

....

16 Handling data 2

1 Two different sets of integers, X and Y, are summarised in the following tables.

X	Frequency
$0 \leq x < 5$	1
$5 \leq x < 10$	3
$10 \leq x < 15$	4
$15 \leq x < 20$	2
$20 \leq x < 25$	2

Y	Frequency
$0 \leq y < 5$	1
$5 \leq y < 10$	3
$10 \leq y < 15$	4
$15 \leq y < 20$	2
$20 \leq y < 25$	2

Both sets of integers have the same modal class and the same highest value, but

- X has a lower mode than Y
- X has a higher range than Y
- X has a higher median than Y.

These are the integers in Y.

$$3, 6, 7, 9, 10, 10, 10, 14, 16, 16, 22, 24$$

Write down a possible set of integers in X. **[3 marks]**

....

....

Answer _____

2 Braxton Town has two strikers, Gary and Tom. A striker's job is to score goals.
At the end of the season a prize is presented to the best striker.

Here are statistics for each striker.
The mean and range are for the number of goals scored per game.

	Gary	Tom
Mean	2	2.2
Range	2	5

Which striker should be presented with the prize?
Use the statistics and explain what these say about
the players' performance. **[4 marks]**

....

....

....

....

....

....

....

3 This table summarises the ages of people living in a block of 8 flats. No one in the flats is over 90 years old.

Age (a, years)	Frequency
$0 < a \leq 10$	3
$10 < a \leq 20$	2
$20 < a \leq 40$	5
$40 < a \leq 60$	6
$60 < a \leq 90$	4

a Jenny works out an estimate of the mean age of these people.

$10 \times 3 = 30$

$20 \times 2 = 40$

$40 \times 5 = 200$

$60 \times 6 = 360$

$90 \times 4 = 360$

Total age $= 30 + 40 + 200 + 360 + 360 = 990$

Mean age $= 990 \div 20 = 49.5$ years

Is Jenny's estimate of the mean age likely to be correct, too low or too high? Explain your answer fully. **[2 marks]**

Likely to be _____ because _____

_____

_____

b Calculate the mean age of the people living in the flats. **[2 marks]**

....

....

Answer _____ years

4 Amrit plays a new game.

He records his best score each week, but the score for week 9 is smudged.

Week	1	2	3	4	5	6	7	8	9	10
Score	50	70	68	74	78	68	78	84	⬤	88

The first eight results are shown on this time-series graph.

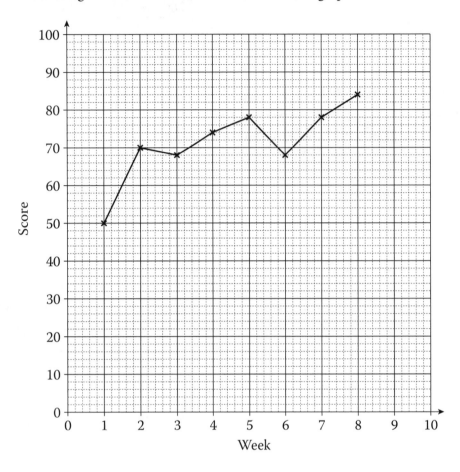

a Plot the score for week 10 on the time-series graph. **[1 mark]**

b Estimate Amrit's score for week 9 and explain, referring to the graph, why it may not be correct. **[2 marks]**

_____

_____

5 Lisa competes in the modern heptathlon. For each practice her coach records her times, in seconds, for the 100 m hurdles and the 200 metres.

These are plotted on the scatter graph.

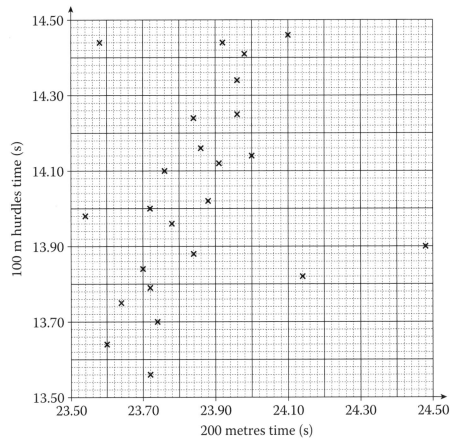

a In which of these two events does Lisa perform better?

Justify your choice by referring to the graph. **[1 mark]**

_____ because _____

_____

b In one practice Lisa ran her best time in the 200 metres but sustained a minor injury in the 100 m hurdles.

What was her 100 m hurdle time? **[1 mark]**

Answer _____ s

c When Lisa runs the 100 m hurdles in 13.85 seconds she scores 1000 points.
When she runs the 200 metres in 23.80 seconds she scores 1000 points.
Lisa only just managed to score 1000 points in the 200 metres at an event.
Use the graph to decide whether she also scored 1000 points in the 100 m hurdles at this event.
Show how you decide. **[1 mark]**

_____ because _____

_____

17 Calculations 2

1. A sphere has a surface area of π cm². Work out the volume of the sphere.

   Leave your answer in terms of π. **[5 marks]**

   ....

   ....

   ....

   ....

   ....

   ....

   ....

   ....

   ....

   ....

   Answer _____ cm³

2. Here are two rectangles, A and B.

   All measurements are in centimetres.

   A ⬜ $\sqrt{k}$ B ⬜ $\sqrt{8}$ Not to scale

   $\sqrt{10}$ $\sqrt{5}$

   In each case below, find an integer value for k and show that it is correct.

   Do not use a calculator. **[4 marks]**

   a The area of A is less than the area of B.

   ....

   ....

   ....

   ....

   $k =$ _____

   because _____

b The area of *A* is equal to the area of *B*.

....

....

....

....

$k = $ _____

because _____

3 There are roughly 6.41×10^7 people alive in the UK today.

Each person uses about 181 litres of water per day.

1 cubic metre $= 10^3$ litres.

Water costs approximately £2.34 per cubic metre.

Work out how much money is paid for water usage in the UK in a year.

Give your answer in pounds, correct to 3 significant figures and written in standard form. **[3 marks]**

....

....

....

....

....

....

....

....

....

....

£ _____

4 A mixed fraction, expressed in its lowest terms, is in the form $a\dfrac{b}{c}$.

The fraction is halved and then $\dfrac{3}{4}$ is added.

The result is $1\dfrac{9}{20}$.

Without using a calculator, and showing all your working, find the values of a, b and c. **[5 marks]**

....

....

....

....

....

....

....

....

....

$a = $ _____

$b = $ _____

$c = $ _____

5 Solve the equation $2x - \sqrt{3} = \sqrt{6}$, leaving square roots in your working and answer. **[2 marks]**

....

....

....

....

Answer _____

6 The ancient Greeks thought that a perfect rectangle had sides in the ratio $1 : \frac{1+\sqrt{5}}{2}$.

a Is this rectangle a perfect rectangle?
Show how you decide. **[3 marks]**

11 cm

6.5 cm

....

....

....

....

....

Answer _____

b The value $\frac{1+\sqrt{5}}{2}$ can be used to calculate a term in the Fibonacci sequence.

1, 1, 2, 3, 5, 8, . . .

The expression for the nth term is

$$\frac{\left(\frac{1+\sqrt{5}}{2}\right)^{n} - \left(1 - \left(\frac{1+\sqrt{5}}{2}\right)\right)^{n}}{\sqrt{5}}$$

Show that the formula gives the correct value for the 10th term in the Fibonacci sequence. **[3 marks]**

....

....

....

....

....

....

....

....

30 minutes

18 Graphs 2

1 Gary worked out the areas of some squares.

   He plotted the area and side length of each square.

   Use these axes to sketch the two graphs Gary could get from his data.

   Label the axes for each graph.   **[4 marks]**

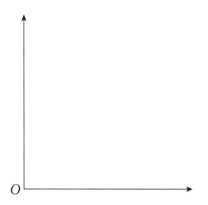 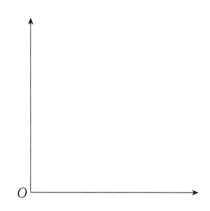

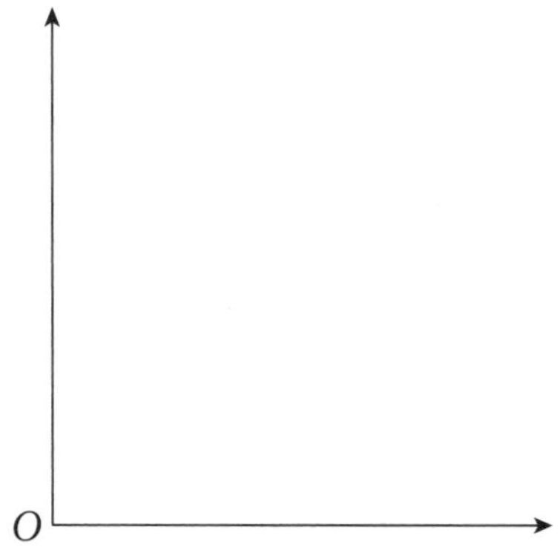

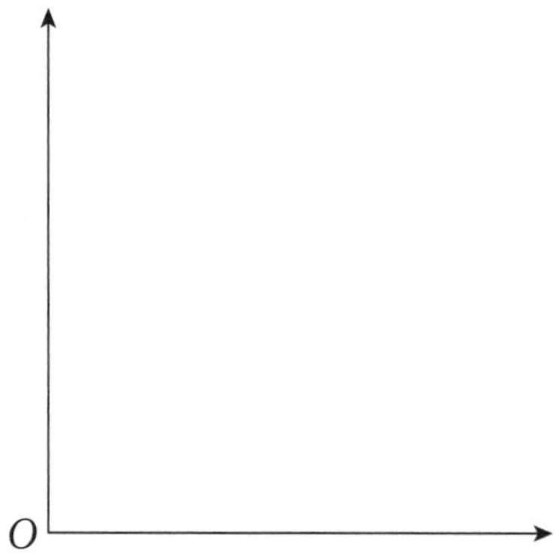

2 This is the graph of $y = \dfrac{x^3}{5} + 4x$.

   Draw a suitable line on the graph that could be used to solve $\dfrac{x^3}{5} + 4x = 5$.

   Label the point where your line meets an axis.   **[1 marks]**

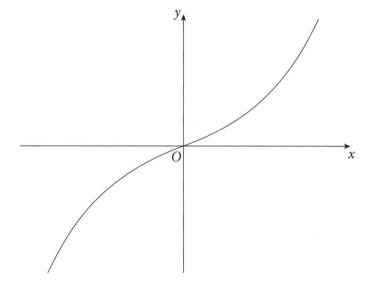

3 The formula $h = 1.5 \sin(30t) + 2.4$ models the height, in metres, of the tide above mean sea level in Brackland, t hours after midnight on 15th June 2015.

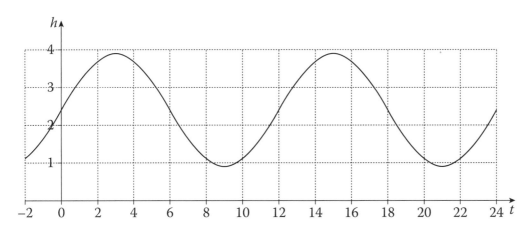

a Explain what the part of the graph between $t = -2$ and $t = 0$ means. **[1 marks]**

....

....

....

Jim knows the water level must be at least 3.5 m above mean sea level for successful fishing.

b On 15th June 2015, find when Jim can fish successfully. **[2 marks]**

....

....

....

In Copbourne, a similar formula for the height of the tide is $h = 2.4 \sin(30t) + 1.5$.
Gill watches the tide in Copbourne.

c Write down two differences Gill would notice between the tide in Brackland and the tide in Copbourne.

Use figures to support your answers where possible. **[3 marks]**

....

....

....

....

....

4 a Complete this table of values for the function $y = x^2 - 4x - 1$. [2 marks]

....

....

....

....

x	−1	0	1	2	3	4	5
y					−4		

b Draw the graph of $y = x^2 - 4x - 1$ for $-1 \leq x \leq 5$. [2 marks]

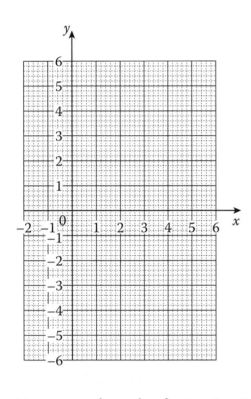

c Use your graph to solve $x^2 - 4x - 1 = -3$. [2 marks]

....

....

Answer _____

d **i** Jess uses the graph to solve $x^2 - 4x - 1 = k$ for a value of k and finds that she has exactly one solution.

What value of k did Jess use? **[1 mark]**

....

....

Answer _____

ii Jess now uses the graph to solve $x^2 - 4x - 1 = -6$.

What should her answer be? **[1 mark]**

....

....

Answer _____

5 **a** On the axes below sketch the graphs of $y = x^3$ and $y = \dfrac{1}{x}$. **[4 marks]**

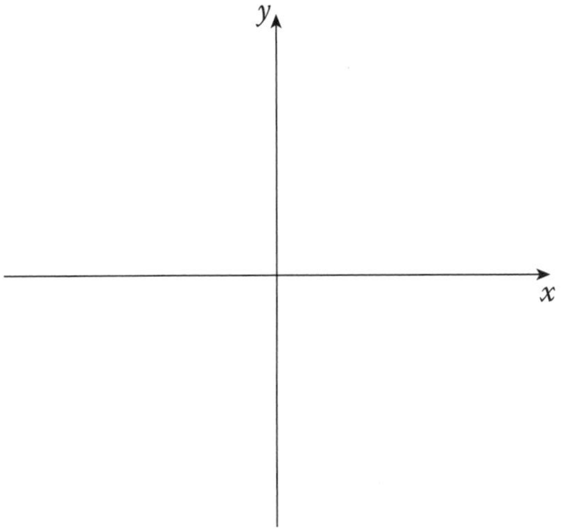

b By referring to your graphs, explain how many solutions the equation $x^3 = \dfrac{1}{x}$ has. **[2 marks]**

....

....

....

....

Answer _____

_____

19 # Pythagoras and trigonometry

1   Use calculations to decide whether or not this triangle is right-angled.   **[3 marks]**

√2 cm

3 cm

√7 cm

Not to scale

....

....

....

....

Answer _____ because _____

2   In a game of racing cars you can describe the moves of each car with vectors.

The diagram shows the first and last moves for one of the cars in a race.

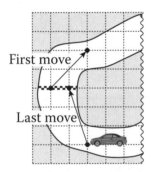

First move

Last move

The vectors for all of the car's moves in the race are added together.

Write down the resultant.

Explain how you got your answer.   **[3 marks]**

Answer $\begin{pmatrix} \\ \end{pmatrix}$ because _____

_____

3 The values for the sines and cosines of angles from 0° to 360° are plotted on this graph.

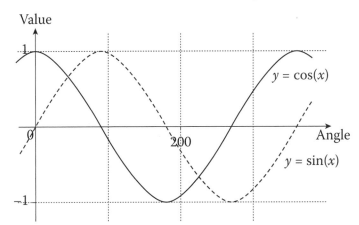

Decide whether each statement is

- always true
- sometimes true
- never true.

Tick the correct box and show evidence when you think the statement is always true or sometimes true.

[4 marks]

a $\sin(x) = \cos(x)$

always true	sometimes true	never true

....

....

b $\sin(x) \geq \cos(x)$

always true	sometimes true	never true

....

....

4 Two rods, one of length 6 cm and the other of length 8 cm, are hinged at their centres.

The rods are rotated and the ends joined by straight lines to form a quadrilateral.

For example:

or

a Calculate the value of maximum perimeter – minimum perimeter. **[5 marks]**

....

....

....

....

....

....

....

....

....

....

....

....

Answer _____ cm

b Calculate the value of the smallest angle between the sides of the quadrilateral when the rods are perpendicular to each other. **[3 marks]**

....

....

....

....

....

Answer _____ °

5 **a** How many vectors are of equal length to $\begin{bmatrix} 3 \\ 5 \end{bmatrix}$, have integer components, but all have different directions?

Show how you decide. **[3 marks]**

Answer _____

b A vector is inclined to the horizontal at 45° and has length 8 units.
Find two possible vectors, leaving square roots in your answer. **[4 marks]**

Answer $\begin{pmatrix} \end{pmatrix}$ and $\begin{pmatrix} \end{pmatrix}$

20 Combined events

1 The Venn diagram shows two sets A and B.

The elements of the sets are in the range 18 to T.

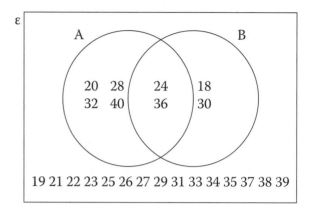

a Write down the value of T. **[1 mark]**

Answer _____

b Write the conditions for a number to be in **[1 mark]**

i set A

_____

ii set B. **[1 mark]**

_____

c Each integer from 1 to T is written on a separate piece of paper.

One piece of paper is selected at random.

Find the probability that the number is a member of A ∩ B. **[2 marks]**

....

....

Answer _____

2 Stacey's shop sells lots of different wood-screws.

Here are some of them described as sets.

Set A: screws that have countersunk heads.
Set B: screws that have round heads.
Set C: screws that are brass.
Set D: screws that are steel.
Set E: screws that are less than 25 mm in length.

Countersunk   Round head

a Andrew buys some screws that are in A ∩ C.

Describe the type of screws Andrew has bought. **[1 mark]**

_____

b Write down two combinations of sets that will be empty.

Explain why each combined set is empty. **[2 marks]**

_____

_____

_____

_____

_____

3 Choy asked some people which football team they supported.

The results are shown in the table.

Team	Arsenal	Liverpool	Chelsea	Bolton	Manchester United	Other clubs
Percentage of people supporting	15%	20%	18%	22%	17%	8%

Decide whether each statement is likely to be true and give a reason for your decision. **[4 marks]**

Choy says

a 'All the people I asked supported a football club'.

_____ because _____

_____

b 'The probability that a person from the UK, picked at random, is a Bolton supporter is 0.22'.

_____ because _____

_____

4   Three fair discs, each with the number 1 on one side and the number 2 on the other, are spun.

The three numbers showing are added together.

Gill says

'There are four possible totals'.

'You are equally likely to get any of the totals'.

'The probability of any of the totals is $\frac{1}{4}$'.

What errors has Gill made?

Show how you decide and give correct probabilities for each different total.   **[6 marks]**

....

....

....

....

....

....

....

....

....

....

....

....

....

....

....

....

....

5   When it rains, Joan gets a lift to school on 80% of these days.

When it is not raining, Joan walks to school 90% of these days.

The tree diagram shows this situation.

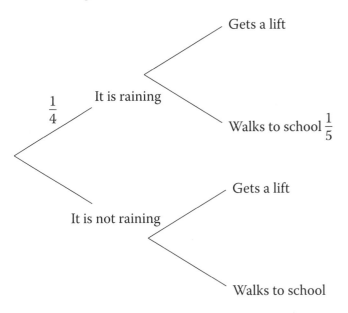

Joan goes to school on 200 days of the year.

On how many of these days can Joan expect to walk to school?   **[7 marks]**

....

....

....

....

....

....

....

....

....

....

....

....

Answer _____ days

21 Sequences

1   Charlotte is making necklaces from black and white beads.

At each end she puts a black bead, and in between she puts groups of 3 white beads separated by another black bead.

For example:

This necklace has 4 black beads and 9 white beads.

a   Sketch the necklace with 6 black beads.   **[1 mark]**

b   If Charlotte used 10 black beads to make a necklace

   i   how many white beads would she use   **[1 mark]**

   ....

   ....

                                                                    Answer _____

   ii   how many beads would she use altogether?   **[1 mark]**

   ....

   ....

                                                                    Answer _____

c   Write an expression for the total number of beads Charlotte uses when she makes
   a necklace with n black beads.   **[2 marks]**

   ....

   ....

                                                                    Answer _____

2 **a** Rick starts a sequence with the number 32. This is the first term.

The difference between successive terms in the sequence is –3.

In what position in the sequence is the first negative term? **[3 marks]**

....

....

....

....

Answer _____

b The first term in Anna's sequence is 3.4×10^3.

The difference between successive terms is –75.

In what position in the sequence is the first negative term and what is its value? **[4 marks]**

....

....

....

....

....

....

....

....

....

Position _____ Value _____

3 The Fibonacci sequence of numbers starts with 0, 1, and then each number is found by adding the two previous numbers.

You can label the Fibonacci numbers F_1, F_2, F_3, etc.

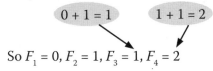

0 + 1 = 1   1 + 1 = 2

So $F_1 = 0$, $F_2 = 1$, $F_3 = 1$, $F_4 = 2$

a Write down F_5 and F_6 and work out F_{10}. **[2 marks]**

....

....

....

$F_5 = $_____, $F_6 = $ _____, $F_{10} = $ _____

The Lucas sequence of numbers has the same rule as the Fibonacci numbers but starting with 2, 1. They are given the labels L_1, L_2, L_3, etc.

b Complete this table showing the first 8 Lucas numbers. **[2 marks]**

L_1	L_2	L_3	L_4	L_5	L_6	L_7	L_8
2	1	3	4				

3 = 2 + 1   4 = 1 + 3

c Write down the sequence of numbers formed by adding a Lucas number to the next-but-one Lucas number. For example $L_1 + L_3 = 2 + 3 = 5$ **[2 marks]**

$L_1 + L_3$	5
$L_2 + L_4$	
$L_3 + L_5$	10
$L_4 + L_6$	
$L_5 + L_7$	
$L_6 + L_8$	

← 3 + 7 = 10

d What type of numbers are made by adding a Lucas number to the next-but-one Lucas number? **[1 mark]**

Answer _____

_____

e   Write a formula to show the connection between $L_n + L_{n+2}$ and F_n.   **[2 marks]**

....

....

....

Answer _____

f   Investigate the sequence formed by $F_{n-2} + F_{n+2}$.   **[3 marks]**

....

....

....

....

....

....

....

....

....

....

Units and proportionality

1 Jenny has a recipe that requires 15 ounces (oz) of caster sugar.

The supermarket has two different sized packs.

● 500 g for 99p

● 700 g for £1.40

$$\boxed{1 \text{ oz} \simeq 28 \text{ g}}$$

Which pack should Jenny buy? Explain your reasoning. **[5 marks]**

....

....

....

....

....

....

....

....

....

....

_____ because _____

_____

2 This pint glass is 15 cm tall.

A half-pint glass is mathematically similar and has half the capacity.

Calculate the height of the half-pint glass. **[4 marks]**

....

....

....

....

....

Answer _____ cm

3 In rectangle *ABCD*,   *BC*:*BD* = 1:2.   *PQRS* is a rectangle.

Not to scale

Not to scale

Are the two rectangles similar? Show how you decide.   **[4 marks]**

....

....

....

....

....

....

....

4 The table below gives details, to 3 significant figures, on the population and area of some countries.

Country	Population (millions)	Area (miles²)
United Kingdom	62.0	94 100
Singapore	5.08	426
Mongolia	2.67	604 000
Bhutan	2.16	18 000

a Complete these sentences with the names of the appropriate countries.   **[2 marks]**

The population of .... is about 12 times the population of ....

The area of .... is about 5 times the area of ....

b Put the four countries in order of population density, from highest to lowest.

Show your working and make the units clear.   **[4 marks]**

....

....

....

....

....

....

....

Answer _____

_____

5   In an electric circuit with constant potential difference, the current, I amperes, is inversely proportional to the resistance, R ohms.

When the resistance is 3 ohms, the current is 8 amperes.

a   Find an equation connecting I and R.   **[3 marks]**

....

....

....

....

....

....

Answer _____

b   Find the **exact** value of R when I equals R.   **[3 marks]**

....

....

....

....

....

....

Answer _____ ohms